MEDITERRANEAN DIET

MANY DELICIOUS AND MOUTH-WATERING RECIPES FROM THE MEDITERRANEAN TRADITION

JIMMY MARCHI

Table of Contents

Cheese Saganaki

You may see this cheese flambé at a Greek restaurant. Don't try that method at home — leave it to the pros!

Serves 4

Ingredients

¼ pound Greek Kefalotyri cheese (or Italian Pecorino)

2 tablespoons all-purpose flour

2 tablespoons extra-virgin olive oil

1 lemon

1. Slice cheese into ½" thick slices.

2. Put flour in a clear plastic bag. Wet cheese slice under running tap, shake off excess water, and drop into bag. Twist bag shut; shake to coat thoroughly with flour.

3. Heat olive oil in shallow pan on medium-high heat. When oil is hot, place cheese in pan; cook until cheese starts to melt along bottom edge.

4. Carefully turn slice over; cook to melting point again. Remove when golden, repeat with remaining cheese, sprinkle with lemon juice, and serve immediately.

Can I Interest You in an Appetizer?

Whether it's tapas at one end of the Mediterranean, or mezes at the other, there is no mistaking the popularity of numerous small dishes as an entrée among the nations that live in and along the shores of "Earth's Middle Sea."

Kalamarakia (Calamari Rings)

Don't neglect these treats while they are cooking; calamari rings that have cooked too long can become rubbery.

Serves 4

Ingredients

4 large frozen squid tubes

3 heaping tablespoons all-purpose flour

1 heaping tablespoon corn flour

Vegetable oil for frying

Juice of 1 lemon

1. Defrost and wash squid tubes; slice into ring segments approximately ¼" in width.

2. Put flour and corn flour in clear plastic bag; shake to mix thoroughly. Add squid; shake in flour to ensure a complete coating.

3. Heat oil in frying pan over medium heat. Make sure to use enough oil to completely immerse rings for frying.

4. Loop some floured ring segments over the handle of a wooden spoon, until you have a good batch for frying; add rings to oil one by one in a clockwise fashion until pan is full. Keep an eye on the time — at the 2½ minute mark, start removing rings in clockwise order from your starting point in the pan.

5. Place cooked rings on plate lined with paper towels to drain until all squid has been cooked. Serve immediately. Be sure to sprinkle the fried calamari liberally with fresh-squeezed lemon juice and serve it with either scorthalia or tzatziki.

Sfougato (Aegean Omelette)

Eggs only for breakfast? Not in the Mediterranean diet! Serve this meal in the morning, afternoon, or even for dinner. It's very common for Greeks to have eggs anytime!

Serves 4
⌒⌐

Ingredients
1 cooking onion, finely diced

4 tablespoons all-purpose flour

¼ cup bread crumbs

2 tablespoons fresh mint, finely chopped

½ cup crumbled Greek feta cheese

Salt and pepper to taste

1 tablespoon dried thyme

6–8 eggs

2 tablespoons extra-virgin olive oil

1. In mixing bowl, add onion, flour, bread crumbs, mint, cheese, salt, pepper, and thyme; mix well.

2. In separate bowl, add eggs; beat well.

3. Add olive oil to large frying pan; heat to medium-high. When oil is hot, add eggs to cheese and bread crumb mixture; combine well then pour into pan.

4. Using wooden spoon, stir until thickened; cook one side 4–5 minutes. Flip it, turn down heat to medium, and cook for another 4–5 minutes, until done.

5. When omelette is cooked, turn off heat and place pan in oven preheated to 350°F for 5 minutes. Serve immediately.

Stuffed Grape Leaves

A traditional staple on any Mediterranean plate, these treats are also known as dolmades.

Yields about 28 pieces

Ingredients
30 medium-sized grape leaves
⅓ cup extra-virgin olive oil
2 onions, diced
1 cup white/Italian style/Arborio rice
¼ cup fresh parsley, chopped
¼ cup fresh mint, chopped
¼ cup fresh dill, chopped
¼ cup pine nuts
1 teaspoon dried oregano
Salt and pepper
½ cup water
Juice of 2 lemons

1. Blanche grape leaves in boiling water until soft; remove from pot and set aside to drain.

2. In frying pan, add 2 tablespoons olive oil; sauté diced onions until soft. Add rice, parsley, mint, dill, pine nuts, oregano, salt, and pepper along with ½ cup water. Cook over medium heat until water is absorbed, about 8–10 minutes or so; remove from heat.

3. Place a grape leaf shiny-side down on flat surface. Put teaspoonful rice mixture in center; fold two sides of leaf inward. Roll up bottom edge to complete small package. Set aside on plate; use up filling using as many leaves as required.

4. Line bottom of deep pan with any remaining leaves; place dolmades closely packed in pan, layering as necessary. Place plate on top of dolmades to prevent them from opening/floating.

5. Add enough boiling water to cover pan contents completely. Pour in lemon juice and remaining olive oil, cover and cook over low heat 30 minutes. Drain any remaining water from pot; set aside to cool slightly before removing. Serve at room temperature and garnish with olive oil and lemon slices.

Amaranth Salad

If you can't find amaranth at your grocery store, you can substitute Swiss chard or arugula.

Serves 4-6
ᕰ

Ingredients
Tender amaranth leaves and shoots (no stalks), a large bunch
Dried Greek oregano
Salt and pepper to taste
Greek extra-virgin olive oil
Wine vinegar

1. Add amaranth leaves and shoots to pot; boil 5–8 minutes, until leaves are a dark green color and shoots are noticeably tender. Remove from pot and place in colander; run under cold water and set aside to drain 15 minutes.

2. Serve with a sprinkling of dried Greek oregano and salt and pepper and drizzle with olive oil and wine vinegar. It is also good served with a dollop of scorthalia over the top.

Roe Salad (Taramosalata/Tarama)

This salad gives you a shot of protein in addition to being very tasty!

Serves 6-8

Ingredients

½ loaf 2-day-old white bread

½ cup carp roe

1 large onion, grated

Juice of 2 lemons

2 cups extra-virgin olive oil

1. Remove outside crust and soak inner bread in water; squeeze well to drain and set aside.

2. Place fish roe in food processor/blender; mix a minute or so to break down eggs.

3. Add grated onion to processor; continue mixing.

4. Add moistened bread in stages to processor/blender; mix well.

5. Slowly add lemon juice and olive oil while constantly mixing. Note: When adding olive oil and lemon juice, add in slow and alternate fashion by first adding some lemon juice then some olive oil and so on, until both are incorporated into the tarama.

6. Refrigerate before serving to firm up the tarama. Garnish with cucumber, tomato slices, and/or olive(s); serve with warm pita bread.

Tzatziki

When you make this yogurt-garlic sauce, make sure you drain the cucumber of all the water you can — it will help the sauce thicken.

Yields 2 ½ cups

Ingredients
½ seedless cucumber
2 cups strained yogurt
3–6 cloves of garlic, pressed or grated
1 tablespoon fresh dill, finely chopped
1 tablespoon extra-virgin olive oil
Pinch of salt
¼ teaspoon white vinegar

1. Peel cucumber; grate onto clean kitchen towel. Wrap; squeeze towel to remove as much water as possible from cucumber. Set aside to drain on fresh towel.

2. In a mixing bowl, combine yogurt, garlic, cucumber, and dill; mix thoroughly until smooth.

3. Add olive oil, salt, and vinegar; mix well once more. Refrigerate at least 1 hour before serving.

Chill Out!
Before the advent of some of the cooler modern conveniences, yogurt was the easiest way to preserve milk's freshness in the warm Mediterranean region.

Tomato and Feta Salad

This salad not only tastes delicious, but with a little style in the presentation, it can also look beautiful!

Serves 4-6

Ingredients

4 large tomatoes, washed and sliced into round slices

¼ pound Greek feta cheese, crumbled

1 teaspoon dried oregano

¼ cup extra-virgin olive oil

2 tablespoons balsamic vinegar

Fresh-ground black pepper

1. Wash and slice tomatoes into rounds approximately ¼" thick. Arrange slices in a slightly overlapping circle pattern on large presentation platter.

2. Cover tomatoes with layer of feta cheese, making sure to spread cheese over all tomato slices then sprinkle oregano over top of the cheese.

3. Combine olive oil and balsamic vinegar; pour over cheese and tomatoes. Sprinkle with fresh-ground pepper and serve.

All in Good Time
Traditional eating patterns are based on seasonal availability of fresh ingredients and do not rely on canning, preservatives, and refrigeration.

No-Pastry Cheese Pie

Also called tyropita, this dish calls for some Greek cheeses that you can find at a specialty cheese shop.

Serves 6

Ingredients
4 eggs

1½ cups grated kefalograviera (saganaki) cheese

1½ cups grated graviera cheese

1 cup strained/pressed yogurt

1 cup all-purpose flour

1⁄3 cup extra-virgin olive oil

1 teaspoon dried oregano

¼ teaspoon fresh-ground pepper

¼ cup dry bread crumbs

1. Preheat oven to 350°F.

2. In large mixing bowl, beat eggs. Add cheeses, yogurt, flour, all of the olive oil (except 1 tablespoonful), oregano, and pepper; mix thoroughly.

3. Grease shallow baking pan with a tablespoonful of olive oil. Evenly sprinkle bread crumbs to cover bottom; pour in and spread mixture evenly.

4. Bake 50–60 minutes, until top is slightly browned. Let cool slightly before cutting to serve.

Spanakotyropita

This dish is better known as spinach and phyllo dough, and is a great appetizer.

Yields approximately 20 pieces

Ingredients
1 package commercial phyllo
2 pounds fresh spinach
½ cup fresh dill, finely chopped
½ cup fennel leaves, finely chopped
2 green onions, diced
2 large leeks, white part only, thinly sliced
½ cup extra-virgin olive oil
1 pound Greek feta cheese, crumbled
2 eggs, lightly beaten
Salt and fresh-ground pepper to taste

1. Preheat oven to 350°F.

2. Wash spinach well; chop coarsely and set aside to drain well. Wash, drain, chop, and combine dill and fennel in mixing bowl.

3. In large frying pan, sauté leeks and diced green onions in 2 tablespoons olive oil until soft; set aside in mixing bowl 10 minutes to cool. Add dill, fennel, feta, eggs, salt, and pepper; mix thoroughly.

4. Spread phyllo sheet. Lightly brush entirely with olive oil; spread line of cheese and vegetable mix along length of one edge. Roll lengthwise into long cigar shape with filling inside. Curl each cigar-shaped package into spiral; place on lightly greased baking sheet.

5. Bake 45 minutes, until golden brown. Serve hot or cold.

Revithosoupa (Chickpea Soup)

Canned chickpeas are available in your grocery store, and they work just fine for this recipe.

Serves 4

Ingredients
1 pound dried chickpeas
Salt and pepper to taste
Several strands of saffron (optional)
2 finely chopped onions
1 cup extra-virgin olive oil
1 teaspoon dried oregano
Juice of 1 lemon
2 tablespoonfuls of chopped parsley

1. Soak chickpeas overnight in double their volume of water.

2. In large pan, add drained chickpeas, salt, pepper, saffron, onions, olive oil, oregano, and enough water to cover chickpeas about 1".

3. Cover and simmer 2 hours, stirring occasionally, until chickpeas are soft and tender. Note: you may need to add some more water if you have to cook them longer than 2 hours, as dried chickpeas generally take longer to cook through.

4. Serve hot or cold with lemon juice. Garnish with chopped parsley and a lemon wedge.

"So, How Was Your Day?"

In Mediterranean countries, meals mean sitting at a proper table with family or friends, not a sandwich at your desk in front of your computer.

Avgolemono (Egg-Lemon Soup)

If you have no orzo pasta in your cabinet, you can use an equal amount of white rice instead.

Serves 4

Ingredients

8 cups chicken stock

1 large carrot, peeled and sliced into discs

1 medium-sized potato, peeled and cut into small cubes

Salt and pepper

½ cup orzo pasta

3 eggs

Juice of 2 lemons

1. In large pot, bring stock to boil. Add carrots, potatoes, salt, and pepper; cover and simmer 15 minutes.

2. Add orzo to pot; cover and cook another 10–12 minutes.

3. While soup is simmering, prepare egg-lemon sauce. Beat eggs well in mixing bowl; in a slow stream add lemon juice while briskly whisking eggs to incorporate citrus thoroughly. Using ladle, take 2 cups hot broth from pot and slowly add to egg-lemon sauce while whisking continuously.

4. When pasta has cooked, uncover pot and slowly pour in egg-lemon sauce while stirring as soup simmers.

Cover pot and turn off heat; allow to stand 5 minutes before serving.

Souper Dinner!

Whether in Greece, Turkey, Italy, Morocco, Spain, Israel, or neighboring countries, a soup or broth can often be the main meal of the day.

Tahini Soup

No tahini at your local supermarket? Try a Middle Eastern specialty store.

Serves 4-6

∽

Ingredients

4–5 pints water

2 cups orzo pasta

Salt and pepper

½ cup tahini

Juice of 2 lemons

1. Bring water to boil in large pot. Add pasta, salt, and pepper; stir well. Cover and simmer until cooked, about 10 minutes. Remove pot from heat.

2. Add tahini to mixing bowl; slowly add lemon juice while whisking constantly. Once lemon juice has been incorporated, take about ½ cup hot broth from pot and slowly add to tahini-lemon mixture while whisking, until creamy smooth.

3. Pour mixture into pot with pasta; mix well. Serve immediately.

Lentil Soup

Toss a few kalamata olives on this soup as garnish, and your guests may never make it to the entrée.

Serves 4

Ingredients

1 pound (2 cups) dry lentils

1 medium-sized onion, finely chopped

1 large carrot, peeled and grated

4 whole garlic cloves

1 cup minced and sieved tomatoes (fresh or canned)

1 teaspoon dried rosemary

2 bay leaves

½ cup extra-virgin olive oil

1. Soak lentils overnight in cold water. Rinse and add to large pot of boiling water 10 minutes; drain water. Add 6 pints fresh water; bring to boil.

2. Add onion, carrot, garlic, tomatoes, rosemary, bay leaves, and olive oil to pot; cover and cook 1 hour, or until lentils are tender. Remove bay leaves and serve hot or cold.

Simplicity is Best

Traditional Mediterranean food cultures are based on simple nonprocessed foods like fruits, vegetables, nuts, seeds, legumes, grains, olive oil, and wine.

Bulgur Pligouri

Walnuts and almonds make a good garnish for this dish, but feel free to use whatever you find tasty.

Serves 4
∽

Ingredients
1 medium-sized onion, diced
1 tablespoon butter
1 tablespoon extra-virgin olive oil
½ cup chopped button mushrooms
1 small handful golden raisins (sultanas)
¼ cup pine nuts
2 cups vegetable or chicken stock (or water with a bouillon cube)
1 teaspoon ground cumin
Salt and pepper to taste
1 cup medium bulgur
1 tablespoon petimezi (concentrated Greek grape must syrup, called Sapa by Italians) or honey
½ cup roasted chestnuts, peeled and cut in half (approximately 12 chestnuts)
1 teaspoon sesame seeds (raw and/or black)

1. In medium-sized saucepan, sauté onion in butter and olive oil over medium heat until soft, 3 minutes or so.

2. Add mushrooms, raisins, and pine nuts to pan; continue to sauté another 2 minutes, stirring regularly.

3. Add stock, cumin, salt, and pepper. Turn heat to medium high and bring to boil; add bulgur and petimezi and cook while stirring well about 3 minutes. [Note: If you cannot find any petimezi, some Greek thyme honey makes a good substitute.]

4. Add chestnuts; stir well. Cover and lower heat to medium-low; allow to simmer 20 minutes or so, until all liquid is absorbed.

5. Uncover and stir thoroughly from the bottom and sides; cover with tea or paper towel before replacing lid (to eliminate any steam-water built up in lid from running back into pan when uncovered for serving). Remove from heat and set aside 10 minutes. Garnish with sesame seeds, both black and raw, then serve.

Makaronada

If you can find myzithra cheese, you'll love the authentic flavor.

Serves 4
෴

Ingredients

1/3 cup extra-virgin olive oil

1 white onion, diced

1 pound lean ground veal

Salt and pepper to taste

¼ cup white wine

1½ cups strained tomato sauce or ¼ cup tomato paste diluted in 1½ cups water

1 medium-sized cinnamon stick

2 bay leaves

1 clove of garlic, whole

1 pound spaghetti-style pasta

Grated myzithra cheese (or Parmesan)

1. Heat olive oil in large pan; sauté onion until soft. Add ground veal; stir well to break up thoroughly. Keep stirring over medium-high heat 5 minutes, or until meat is browned.

2. Once meat is browned, add salt and pepper, wine, and tomato sauce; mix well. Bring to boil.

3. Add cinnamon stick, bay leaves, and garlic clove and cover with sauce; reduce heat to medium-low. Cover

pot, leaving slightly uncovered to allow water to evaporate as steam; simmer 30 minutes. The sauce should reduce so that the water is steamed away and the tomato and cinnamon hinted olive oil is left behind with the meat. When ready, meat will have absorbed all liquid.

4. Boil and strain pasta. Sprinkle generously with grated myzithra cheese; spoon meat sauce over top. Make sure to stir sauce first to get some orange-tinted olive oil in each helping.

Greek Rigatoni

Who says you have to go to Italy to get a delicious plate of pasta?

Serves 4

Ingredients
½ pound rigatoni shape pasta
¾ cup kalamata black olives
10 sundried tomatoes
½ pound Greek feta cheese
1⁄3 cup extra-virgin olive oil
1 tablespoon dried oregano
Fresh-ground black pepper

1. Bring salted water to boil; cook pasta according to directions on package.

2. Pit and chop olives into pieces (not too small). Chop sundried tomatoes into ribbons. Cut feta into small cubes.

3. Heat olive oil in large sauté pan.

4. Drain pasta well; add to heated olive oil in sauté pan. Add feta, and sundried tomatoes; heat through by tossing repeatedly for a couple minutes until cheese just starts to melt.

5. Season with oregano and pepper; give a couple more tosses in pan and serve hot.

Say Cheese!
Feta cheese accounts for well over half of the 27.3 kilos of cheese the average Greek consumes in a year. No other nation eats as much cheese, not even the French.

Lemon Potatoes

Yukon Gold potatoes work best for this recipe, but experiment with your favorite kind.

Serves 4-6

Ingredients

2½ pounds potatoes, washed and peeled
½ cup Greek extra-virgin olive oil
Salt and pepper to taste
Juice of 2 lemons
1 tablespoon finely shredded lemon rind
1 heaping tablespoon dried oregano

1. Cut potatoes into thin wedges slightly bigger than fries but not too big, as you want them to cook through and crisp slightly on outside.

2. Spray or sprinkle olive oil to coat bottom and sides of deep-walled medium-sized baking pan (stone bakeware works best).

3. Spread potato slices evenly across bottom of pan; liberally sprinkle salt and fresh-ground pepper on top.

4. Add enough water to almost but not quite cover bottom layer of potatoes. Add lemon juice and lemon rind; using your hands, mix potatoes well in pan to ensure an even soaking and help spread salt, pepper, and lemon zest.

5. Pour remaining olive oil over top of potatoes, making sure to cover all of them; sprinkle oregano over everything. Bake approximately 50 minutes in a 375°F oven; mix potatoes well at halfway mark, to guarantee a thorough and even baking. When potatoes are visibly crisping at edges it is time to remove the pan or turn oven off.

Health and Longevity

It has become common knowledge that certain elements of Mediterranean diets, especially olive oil, fresh vegetables, fruits, legumes, fresh fish, nuts, and cereals offer considerable health benefits toward a vigorous and lengthy life.

Fassolakia Moraïtika (Braised Green Beans)

If you have one, a bean slicer can make this recipe that much easier!

Serves 4

Ingredients

2 pounds fresh green beans, washed and trimmed

½ cup extra-virgin olive oil

1 medium-sized cooking onion, finely chopped

1 large or 2 medium-sized red skin potatoes, washed and cut into eighths (optional)

1½ cups fresh tomato juice, sauce, or strained tomato pulp

4 tablespoons chopped fresh mint

Salt and pepper to taste

1. Wash and clean beans by trimming ends and removing strings.

2. Heat olive oil in cooking pot over medium-high heat; reduce heat to medium and sauté onion until slightly softened and translucent.

3. Add beans to pot; stir well to mix with olive oil and onion. Cover and let simmer 10 minutes.

4. Uncover and stir; add potatoes, tomato juice, mint, salt, and pepper along with 1 cup water. Stir well, but make sure potato pieces end up under beans.

5. Bring to boil; reduce heat to medium-low and partially cover pot, leaving it slightly open to allow steam to

escape so sauce can reduce. Let simmer 45 minutes to 1 hour, or until beans and potatoes are tender enough to cut with fork. Stir occasionally if necessary, but avoid adding water to cover, as this will result in a runny, thin sauce; this dish is not meant to be soupy.

Greek Baked Vegetable Medley

Don't just go by the recipe — throw your favorite veggies into this medley!

Serves 4

Ingredients
2 large eggplants, cubed

2 zucchini, cubed

2 large potatoes, cubed

2 large parsnips, peeled and thickly sliced

2 large carrots, peeled and thickly sliced

1 pound white button mushrooms, thickly sliced

1 large yellow onion, sliced

1 large red pepper, cut into strips

6 garlic cloves, cut in half

½ cup extra-virgin olive oil

1 tablespoon fresh rosemary, finely chopped

½ tablespoon dried oregano

Salt and pepper to taste

1. Preheat oven to 400°F.

2. Wash eggplant and cut into small cubes; place in colander and sprinkle with salt. Place colander over plate and let stand 30 minutes to drain bitter juices.

3. Wash and cut remaining vegetables; set aside until eggplant has drained.

38

4. Rinse eggplant and combine all vegetables and garlic in large baking dish; add olive oil and mix well. Sprinkle with rosemary, oregano, salt, and pepper; add enough water to cover bottom half of baking dish and contents.

5. Bake uncovered 50–60 minutes, or until water has been absorbed. Make sure to stir vegetables at least once halfway through cooking time, or as needed.

6. Serve warm.

Chickpea Rissoles

Serve these rissoles alone, or with a tomato sauce or your favorite dip.

Serves 4
∽

Ingredients
1 pound chickpeas (soaked overnight if dry)

1 egg

1 tablespoon dried oregano or finely chopped fresh

3 tablespoons finely chopped fresh mint

3 tablespoons flour

1 teaspoon pepper

½ teaspoon salt

3 tablespoons bread crumbs

Vegetable oil for deep-frying

1. Boil chickpeas 30 minutes, or until soft; drain and purée with egg, oregano, mint, flour, pepper, and salt.

2. Scrape chickpea purée into mixing bowl. Add bread crumbs; mix well.

3. Spread sheet of wax paper on counter/cutting board. Spoon about ⅓ of chickpea mixture in an even line along horizontal center of wax paper. Fold over bottom half of wax paper and using the flat of your hand, roll mixture into a long cylindrical shape (similar to using a sushi roller). Cut resulting

cylindrical shape into 3 equal pieces or "sausages." Repeat to use up the rest of chickpea mixture.

4. Place rissoles into sizzling oil; fry 5–6 minutes, making sure to turn often if oil does not completely cover rissoles. Remove with slotted spoon; set on paper towel a few minutes to drain.

"The Fainting Cleric"
The name of the dish "Imam Bayildi" is Turkish for "The Fainting Cleric" and as the legend has it, a certain imam (Muslim religious leader) had just completed a long fast and when this dish was set before him, he was so overcome with the mouth-watering aroma that he fainted.

Black-Eyed Peas with Swiss Chard

If you've never tried Swiss chard, this is a great introduction to the leafy green. It has a bitter taste at first, but makes a great addition to many dishes.

Serves 4
∽

Ingredients
1 cup dry black-eyed peas
2 pounds Swiss chard
Salt and pepper
¼ cup extra-virgin olive oil
1 teaspoon dried oregano
1 lemon

1. Soak peas overnight. Drain and rinse before using.

2. Bring pot of water to boil; simmer peas 15 minutes.

3. Drain water from pot. Add fresh water, olive oil, oregano, and salt and pepper; bring to boil again. Simmer on medium-low heat 30 minutes.

4. Chop Swiss chard leaves into ribbons; add to pot after 30 minutes. Simmer another 5 minutes.

5. Sprinkle with lemon juice. Serve warm or cold.

Roasted Lemon Chicken

Potato wedges can be added to the pan, but if you do add them, make sure you add enough water to cover them. Add a splash of lemon juice and olive oil — yum!

Serves 4

Ingredients
1 whole chicken
Salt and pepper to taste
Juice of 2 lemons, shells retained
2 tablespoons extra-virgin olive oil
1 tablespoon prepared mustard
1 teaspoon dried oregano

1. Preheat oven to 400°F.

2. Wash chicken well inside and out and pat dry. Sprinkle inside and out with salt and pepper and stuff squeezed out lemon halves into cavity. Place chicken breast down on rack in shallow roasting dish. Combine lemon juice, olive oil, mustard, and oregano; brush/pour over entire chicken.

3. Bake 60–70 minutes, making sure to turn chicken over at halfway point and basting it regularly with juices from pan.

4. To test if it's done, prick with fork and see if juices run clear, or test with meat thermometer for 350°F. When

done, turn off oven and cover chicken in aluminum foil. Let rest in warm oven 10 minutes.

5. Serve hot with pan juices.

Lemon History 101

The lemon is not native to the Mediterranean region. It is conjectured to have been brought from Asia sometime around the first or second centuries A.D. A first-century A.D. wall painting in Pompeii is the earliest available evidence of the lemon in Europe.

Stuffed Grilled Chicken Breast

Watch this dish when you're grilling it — if any stuffing drips out, it can cause a flare-up on the grill.

Serves 6

Ingredients

6 large boneless, skinless chicken breasts

1 cup crumbled Greek feta cheese

½ cup finely minced sundried tomatoes

1 teaspoon dried oregano

2 tablespoons extra-virgin olive oil

Salt and pepper

1. Wash chicken breasts well and pat dry with paper towel.

2. In bowl, mix feta with sundried tomatoes and oregano; combine thoroughly.

3. Place each chicken breast on flat surface; using sharp paring knife, carefully slit top edge of each breast and make deep incision that runs within length of each breast. Be careful not to pierce any holes that would allow stuffing to seep out while grilling.

4. Use small spoon to stuff an equal portion of cheese mixture into each breast; use poultry pins or toothpicks to close openings.

5. Sear breasts in heated frying pan with olive oil, approximately 2–3 minutes per side.

6. Sprinkle with salt and pepper; cook on prepared grill over high heat about 15 minutes, approximately 8 minutes per side. Serve immediately.

Chicken or the Egg?
The question of which came first, the chicken or the egg, was a popular after-dinner conversation topic at ancient Greek drinking parties (symposia).

Chicken Galantine

Serve this tender chicken with a roasted eggplant; the flavors will complement each other perfectly.

Serves 6

∼

Ingredients

1 small whole chicken

1 shallot

2 cloves garlic

¼ cup pistachio nuts

8 dates

½ pound ground chicken

1 egg white

1 teaspoon dried oregano

1 teaspoon dried marjoram

Fresh-cracked black pepper, to taste

Kosher salt, to taste

1. Preheat oven to 325°F.

2. Carefully remove all the skin from the chicken by making a slit down the back and loosening the skin with your fingers (keep the skin intact as much as possible); set aside the chicken and the skin. Remove the breast from bone. Chop the shallot and mince the garlic. Chop the nuts and dates.

3. Mix together the ground chicken, egg white, nuts, dates, shallots, garlic, oregano, marjoram, pepper, and salt.

4. Lay out the skin, then lay the breast lengthwise at the center. Spoon the ground chicken mixture on top, and fold over the rest of skin. Place in a loaf pan and bake for 1½ to 2 hours (when the internal temperature of the loaf reaches 170° F, it's done). Let cool, then slice.

Grilled Duck with Fruit Salsa

Moulard duck breast is the best kind for this recipe, but you can use another type if you prefer.

Serves 6
∾

Ingredients
1 plum
1 peach
1 nectarine
1 red onion
3 sprigs mint
Fresh-cracked black pepper, to taste
1 tablespoon olive oil
1 teaspoon chili powder
1½ pounds boneless duck breast

1. Preheat grill. Dice the plum, peach, nectarine, and onion. Mince the mint. Toss together the fruit, onion, mint, and pepper.

2. Mix together the oil and chili powder. Dip the duck breast in the oil, and cook to desired doneness on grill.

3. Slice duck on the bias and serve with spoonful of salsa.

Leek and Celery Pork

Toss the green stalks of leeks for this recipe and just use the white ends.

Serves 4

Ingredients

2 pounds pork shoulder, chopped into cubes
1 onion, finely chopped
½ cup extra-virgin olive oil
½ cup white wine
2 cups water
2 pounds leeks
1 cup finely chopped celery
1 cup tomatoes, diced and sieved (fresh or canned)
1 teaspoon dried oregano
Salt and fresh-ground pepper

1. Wash pork well; chop into cubes and set aside to drain.

2. In deep-walled pot, sauté onion in olive oil until slightly soft; add pork and brown thoroughly.

3. Add wine to pot; bring to boil then cover and simmer 15 minutes, stirring regularly. Remove pork; cover to keep warm and set aside.

4. Add water to pan along with leeks and celery; bring to boil and simmer 30 minutes over medium heat.

5. Return pork to pot along with tomatoes, oregano, salt, and pepper; stir well. Bring to boil and continue to simmer until sauce is reduced and thickened, approximately 8–10 minutes. Serve immediately.

Olive You!
The oldest olive tree in the world is situated in Vouves, Crete, and is thought to be approximately 3,500 years old.

White Wine Pork Chops

Boneless chops work fine for this recipe, but it works best with bone-in pork chops.

Serves 4

Ingredients
4 thick-cut pork chops
½ cup extra-virgin olive oil
1 cup white wine
1 tablespoon dried oregano
Salt and pepper to taste

1. Rinse pork chops well and pat dry with paper towel.

2. Place 2 tablespoons olive oil in frying pan; lightly brown pork chops.

3. Put remaining olive oil in fresh pan and turn heat to medium-high. Cook pork chops 3–4 minutes per side, making sure to turn them over at least once.

4. Add wine; bring to boil. Turn to medium and simmer 10 minutes, turning meat once.

5. Add ½ cup hot water to pan; bring to boil and let simmer until sauce has reduced. Sprinkle with oregano, salt, and pepper and serve immediately.

Braised Lamb Shoulder

This recipe goes wonderfully with leftover pasta or rice.

Serves 4

∾

Ingredients

1½–2 pounds lamb shoulder

½ cup extra-virgin olive oil

½ cup hot water

2 cups tomatoes, diced and sieved (fresh or canned)

2 bay leaves

4 garlic cloves, peeled and minced

1 cinnamon stick

1 tablespoon dried thyme

Salt and pepper to taste

1. Wash meat well and cut into small pieces; include bones.

2. Heat olive oil in pot; brown meat on all sides.

3. Add water, tomatoes, bay leaves, garlic, cinnamon, thyme, salt, and pepper; cover and bring to boil, then turn heat down to medium-low.

4. Simmer 1½ hours, stirring occasionally.

Braised Beef with Onions

This recipe calls for pearl onions, but you can use any kind of small onion.

Serves 4

Ingredients

½ cup extra-virgin olive oil
2 pounds stewing beef, cubed
2 tablespoons tomato paste, diluted in 2 cups of water
2 tablespoons wine vinegar (or a sweet dessert wine like Madeira or Mavrodaphne)
14–16 pearl onions, peeled
6 garlic cloves, peeled
4 spice cloves
1 small cinnamon stick
1 tablespoon dried oregano
Salt and fresh-ground pepper

1. Add olive oil to large pot. Heat to medium-high; add meat and brown well on all sides by stirring continuously so meat does not stick to bottom of pot.

2. Add tomato paste, wine vinegar, onions, garlic, cloves, cinnamon, oregano, salt, and pepper; mix well and turn heat to high. Bring to boil.

3. Cover and turn heat down to medium-low; simmer approximately 1 hour.

4. Serve immediately, accompanied by fresh bread for sauce.

Stew You Think You Can Cook?

A stifado is essentially an onion-based stew with meat. One can use rabbit, chicken, lamb, pork, beef, or veal in this quintessentially Greek dish. Stifado can even be made with game.

Shrimp Saganaki

A shot of Sambuca or ouzo can be substituted for mastic resin in this recipe.

Serves 4

∾

Ingredients
2 medium-sized onions, diced
¼ cup extra-virgin olive oil
4 garlic cloves, pressed or finely diced
2 cups diced and sieved tomatoes (fresh or canned)
1 roasted red pepper, minced
½ cup water
Salt and pepper to taste
2 tablespoons mastiha liqueur
¼–½ teaspoon ground mastic resin
20–24 large raw shrimp, shelled with tails on
1 cup crumbled Greek feta (optional)

1. Sauté onions in olive oil over medium heat until soft and translucent, 3–5 minutes.

2. Add garlic and stir well 30 seconds. Add tomatoes, red pepper, and water; add salt and pepper to taste and stir well to mix. Bring to boil.

3. Reduce heat only slightly and allow sauce to simmer well 8 minutes; do not cover pan.

4. Add mastiha liqueur and mastic resin to sauce; stir well. Continue to simmer another 2 minutes, stirring a couple more times.

5. Quickly add shrimp; give pan a couple shakes to settle shrimp well into sauce. Cook 2 minutes.

6. Using tongs or fork, quickly turn all shrimp over and cook another minute or so.

7. Remove from heat for serving. A cup of crumbled Greek feta can be added to pan just before removing from heat for serving.

Not So Fast!
According to Greek Orthodox Christian fasting customs, shellfish, octopus, and cuttlefish are considered fast-friendly as they do not contain blood.

Baked Aegean Sole

Feel free to use turbot, halibut, or flounder instead of sole here —
whatever fish you fancy!

Serves 4

Ingredients
8 sole fillets
Salt and pepper to taste
2 lemons
4 tablespoons extra-virgin olive oil
1 teaspoon dried oregano
¼ cup capers
4 tablespoons chopped fresh dill
2 tablespoons chopped fresh green onion (or celery leaves or parsley)

1. Preheat oven to 250°F.

2. Wash fish well under cold water and pat dry with paper towel. Salt and pepper fillets and set aside.

3. Slice 1 lemon into thin slices, then cut slices in half.

4. Pour 2 tablespoons olive oil into baking dish; layer fish and lemon slices alternately.

5. Sprinkle oregano, capers, dill, and onion over fish and lemon slices.

6. Drizzle remaining olive oil and squeeze juice of remaining lemon over everything.

7. Cover and bake 30 minutes.

Baked Tuna

Historians report that tuna fishing has been in operation in Greece since 6000 B.C.!

Serves 4

∾

Ingredients

4 center-cut tuna fillets, 6–8 ounces each (2 pounds total)

1 large yellow onion, sliced

1 large green pepper, diced

¼ cup extra-virgin olive oil

2 cloves garlic, minced or pressed

2 tablespoons chopped parsley

1 teaspoon dried marjoram (or ½ teaspoon dried oregano)

Salt and fresh-ground pepper to taste

2 cups peeled tomatoes, finely minced (canned tomatoes are fine)

½ cup water

1. Preheat oven to 400°F.

2. Wash tuna steaks well and set aside.

3. In large frying pan, heat 2 tablespoons olive oil on medium-high. Sauté onion and green pepper until soft.

4. Add garlic, parsley, marjoram, salt, and pepper; stir over heat another minute or so.

5. Add tomatoes and water; bring to boil. Lower heat to medium-low and simmer 15–20 minutes.

6. Place tuna steaks in baking dish along with remaining olive oil, making sure to coat the tuna with the oil; pour sauce over top. Bake uncovered 45 minutes. Serve immediately, spooning some sauce over each portion and garnishing with chopped fresh parsley.

Grilled Sea Bass

Sea bass can easily be overcooked, so be sure to remove the fish from the grill when it gets flaky.

Serves 4

∾

Ingredients

4 whole sea bass (1½ pounds each), gutted and scaled

Salt and pepper

4 lemons

¼ cup extra-virgin olive oil

1 teaspoon dried oregano

1 cup fresh parsley, finely chopped

1. Wash fish well inside and out. Using sharp knife, cut several diagonal slits on both sides of each fish. Sprinkle with salt and pepper, including inside cavity, and set aside.

2. Squeeze juice from 2 lemons and mix with olive oil and oregano.

3. Slice remaining 2 lemons into thin slices and stuff each fish with chopped parsley and several lemon slices.

4. Brush both sides of each fish liberally with olive oil and lemon mixture and set aside 10 minutes.

5. Heat grill to medium heat; brush grilling rack with oil. Place fish on hot rack and close grill cover.

6. Cook 15 minutes, until fish flakes easily. Brush with remaining olive oil and lemon mixture and serve hot.

Sautéed Octopus with Wine

When cooking octopus, be sure to remove the beak, eyes, and ink sac before cooking.

Serves 4

Ingredients
1 large octopus
1 tablespoon white vinegar
½ cup extra-virgin olive oil
3 onions, sliced
4 tomatoes, diced and sieved (fresh or canned)
1 cup white wine
2 bay leaves
1 teaspoon whole peppercorns
Salt and pepper
½ cup drained capers
¼ cup water

1. Place octopus in saucepan with vinegar; cover and simmer over a low heat until soft, approximately 15–20 minutes. Remove and cut into small pieces.

2. Heat olive oil in frying pan and sauté onions until soft.

3. Add tomatoes, wine, bay leaves, peppercorns, salt, and pepper; simmer 15 minutes.

4. Add octopus, capers, and water; simmer until sauce has thickened. Serve hot.

Milk Pie

Use 2 percent milk or higher to increase flavor in this delicious dessert.

Serves 6

Ingredients

5 cups milk

½ cup butter

1 cup sugar

1 cup fine semolina

3 eggs

Ground cinnamon or icing sugar for sprinkling

1. Preheat oven to 350°F.

2. On stovetop, bring milk almost to boil in saucepan. Add butter, sugar, and semolina, making sure to stir continuously until thick crème is formed. Turn off heat and let stand a couple minutes to cool slightly.

3. Beat eggs and add to thickened mixture; whisk well.

4. Butter or oil sides and bottom of pie dish or other high-walled oven pan. Pour in mixture; bake approximately 1 hour, until top has browned. Turn off oven but do not remove pie for another 15 minutes.

5. Once pie is removed from oven, let stand a couple hours. Serve topped with icing sugar or cinnamon. Can also be topped with fruit preserve or jam of your choosing.

Greek Rice Pudding

You can serve this dish warm or cold, but nothing beats a cool bowl of this on a sunny day!

Serves 6-8

Ingredients
8 cups milk
1 cup Arborio rice
1½ cups sugar
1 teaspoon real vanilla extract
1 tablespoon finely shredded citrus zest (orange, lemon, or lime)
2 egg yolks
¼ cup cold milk
1 tablespoon corn flour (optional)
1 teaspoon ground cinnamon

1. In pot over moderately high heat, bring milk to slight boil. Add rice and stir well until boil returns. Reduce heat to medium-low and gently simmer uncovered 30 minutes. Make sure to stir regularly so milk does not congeal or stick to sides and/or bottom of pot.

2. Add sugar, vanilla, and citrus rind; continue to simmer and occasionally stir another 10 minutes.

3. Beat egg yolks with cold milk; whisk in corn flour and mix well.

4. After 10 minutes in Step 2, pour egg yolk mixture into pot; whisk well to incorporate. Simmer another 3–5 minutes, until thick.

5. Remove from heat. Using ladle, spoon out mixture into bowls. Let stand 1 hour to cool. Sprinkle with cinnamon and garnish with curls of shaved citrus rind.

Stuffed Dried Figs

These are a great snack to take on a long car trip, or to pep you up after a long workout.

Serves 4

Ingredients

12 dried figs

24 walnut halves

2 tablespoons thyme honey

2 tablespoons sesame seeds

1. Snip tough stalk ends off figs. For each fig, slice side and open with fingers.

2. Stuff 2 walnut halves inside each fig and fold closed.

3. Arrange figs on platter. Drizzle with honey and sprinkle with sesame seeds to serve.

Byzantine Fruit Salad

If you have a favorite piece of fruit that isn't present in the ingredients list, don't hesitate to add it.

Serves 4

Ingredients
2 apples, peeled and cubed
2 pears, peeled and cubed
Seeds from 1 pomegranate
3 mandarins, peeled and sectioned
½ cup red wine
½ cup Greek anthomelo (blossom honey)

1. Prepare fruits and mix together in medium-sized bowl.

2. Bring wine and blossom honey to boil and let roll for a few minutes to burn off most of the alcohol. Allow to cool 20 minutes.

3. Pour over mixed fruit and refrigerate at least 1 hour. Be sure to stir fruit a few times to ensure sauce covers everything. Serve anytime as a snack or dessert.

Sunrise Bruschetta

Veggies are a huge part of Mediterranean diet meals — even breakfast!

Serves 4

Ingredients

½ loaf of Italian or French bread

½ cup extra-virgin olive oil

¼ cup pesto

1 medium tomato

2 egg whites

2 whole eggs

1 roasted red pepper

¼ cup mozzarella cheese

1. Slice the bread into 4¾" lengthwise pieces. Brush 1 side of each with a bit of the oil; toast on grill. When that side is toasted, brush oil on the other side, flip, and toast that side.

2. Place the toasted bread on a sheet pan and spread with pesto. Peel and chop the tomato; combine it with the eggs. Dice the pepper and shred the cheese.

3. Heat the remaining oil in a sauté pan to medium temperature; add the egg mixture and cook omelet style. Cut the omelet and place on the bread; top with cheese and pepper.

Strata with Bleu Cheese

This dish is meant for breakfast, but makes a great addition to any brunch menu.

Serves 6

Ingredients
3 (1½") slices seedless rye bread
3 (1½") slices pumpernickel bread
½ teaspoon extra-virgin olive oil
2 whole eggs
6 egg whites
¼ cup skim milk
¼ cup plain nonfat yogurt
2 ounces bleu cheese
Fresh-cracked black pepper, to taste

1. Preheat oven to 375ºF.

2. Tear the bread into large pieces. Grease a 2-quart casserole pan with the oil.

3. In a large mixing bowl, beat the eggs and egg whites; add the milk, yogurt, and cheese.

4. Place the bread pieces in the prepared casserole pan, then pour in the egg mixture. Bake for 40 to 50 minutes, until the mixture is set and the top is golden brown. To serve, cut into squares and season with pepper.

Breakfast Pastina

Who says you can't have spaghetti for breakfast? This dish will pep you up on even the slowest morning.

Serves 6

Ingredients
1 whole egg
2 egg whites
3 cups chicken broth (fat removed)
1½ cups pastina
1 ounce fresh Parmesan cheese, grated
Fresh-cracked black pepper, to taste
¼ bunch fresh parsley, chopped

1. Beat the egg and egg whites. Bring the broth to a slow boil in a medium-size saucepot, then add the pastina; stir frequently until almost al dente.

2. Whisk in the eggs, stirring constantly until the eggs are completely cooked and the pasta is al dente. Remove from heat and ladle into bowls. Sprinkle in cheese, pepper, and parsley.

Eggs in Crusty Bread Bowls

On cold weekend mornings, curl up with this hot delight and watch the snow fall.

Serves 6

Ingredients
6 (2") slices Italian bread
1 teaspoon virgin olive oil
2 red peppers, thinly sliced
½ shallot, minced
6 eggs
Fresh-cracked black pepper, to taste
Kosher salt, to taste

1. Cut out large circles from the center of the bread slices; discard the center pieces and set the hollowed-out bread slices aside. Heat half of the oil to medium in a sauté pan. Sauté the peppers and shallots until tender. Remove from heat and drain on paper towel; keep warm.

2. Heat the remaining oil on medium-high heat in a large sauté pan. Place the bread slices in the pan. Crack 1 egg into the hollowed-out center of each bread slice. When the eggs solidify, flip them together with the bread (being careful to keep the egg in place), and cook to desired doneness.

3. To serve, remove from pan and top with the pepper-shallot mixture. Season with pepper and salt.

Israeli Couscous and Fruit Chutney

A yummy meal on its own, this dish can also be a neutral addition to a spicy entrée.

Serves 6

Ingredients

¼ cup medium-diced dried dates

¼ cup medium-diced dried figs

¼ cup medium-diced dried currants

¼ cup slivered almonds

¼ cup strawberry jam

Couscous

2¼ cups fresh orange juice

2¼ cups water

4½ cups couscous

1 teaspoon grated orange rind

2 tablespoons nonfat plain yogurt

1. Mix together all the chutney ingredients; set aside.

2. Bring the orange juice and water to a boil in a medium-size pot. Stir in the couscous, then add the orange rind. Remove from heat immediately, cover, and let stand for 5 minutes. Fluff the mixture with a fork.

3. Serve in bowls with a spoonful of chutney and a dollop of yogurt.

Mascarpone Dumplings

If you like cream cheese, you'll probably like mascarpone! Feel free to add more or use less honey in this recipe, depending on your sweet tooth.

Serves 6

Ingredients
1 cup whole-wheat flour

1 cup all-purpose unbleached flour

¼ cup ground almonds

4 egg whites

3 ounces mascarpone cheese

1 teaspoon extra-virgin olive oil

2 teaspoons apple juice

1 tablespoon butter

¼ cup honey

1. Sift together both types of flour in large bowl. Mix in the almonds. In a separate bowl, cream together the egg whites, cheese, oil, and juice on medium speed with an electric mixer.

2. Combine the flour and egg white mixture with a dough hook on medium speed or by hand until a dough forms.

3. Boil 1 gallon water in medium-size saucepot. Take a spoonful of the dough and use a second spoon to push

it into the boiling water. Cook until the dumpling floats to the top, about 5 to 10 minutes. You can cook several dumplings at once, just take care not to crowd the pot. Remove with a slotted spoon and drain on paper towels.

4. Heat a medium-size sauté pan on medium-high heat. Add the butter, then place the dumplings in the pan and cook until light brown. Place on serving plates and drizzle with honey.

Grilled Tuna Sandwich

This one is a toughie when it comes to leftovers. If you want to make it last, don't put the tuna mixture on the bread until you're ready to eat to avoid sogginess.

Serves 6

Ingredients
1 hard-boiled egg
1 red onion
1 medium apple
¼ teaspoon lemon juice
1 cup water
1 pound cooked or canned tuna
¼ cup chopped walnuts
2 tablespoons extra-virgin olive oil
1 tablespoon balsamic vinegar, or to taste
Kosher salt, to taste
Fresh-cracked black pepper
1 small loaf Italian bread
1 head green or red leaf lettuce

1. Medium-dice the egg and onion. Dice the apple and toss it in the lemon juice and water; drain.

2. Mix together the tuna, egg, onion, apple, nuts, oil, and vinegar; season with salt and pepper. Cut the bread in half lengthwise, then layer the lettuce and mound the tuna mixture on top.

79

3. Wrap the loaf tightly with plastic wrap and refrigerate for 1 hour. Slice into 6 equal portions and serve.

Arugula Flatbread Sandwich

Arugula is a forgotten leafy green that is a delicious addition to many recipes. You can pick it up in your supermarket's produce section.

Serves 6

Ingredients

1 teaspoon olive oil

2 ounces pancetta

3 cups fresh arugula

12 slices flatbread

Fresh-cracked black pepper

1. Heat the oil to medium temperature in a medium-size saucepan. Add the pancetta, and brown.

2. Add the arugula, wilt, and immediately mound on the flatbread; add pepper to taste.

3. Serve with Gorgonzola or your favorite cheese.

Traditional Greek Pita

Feta cheese is a Greek staple, but use it with caution. It has a salty flavor that makes itself known in even small amounts!

Serves 6

Ingredients
2 European cucumbers
1 large red onion
¼ bunch oregano
2 anchovy fillets (optional)
6 pita bread
3 ounces feta cheese
1 tablespoon olive oil
Fresh-cracked black pepper

1. Peel and dice the cucumber and thinly slice the onion. Chop the oregano. Mash the anchovy fillets.

2. Cut a slit into each pita and stuff with cucumber, onion, oregano, and feta.

3. Drizzle with oil and sprinkle with mashed anchovy and black pepper.

Sesame Tuna Carpaccio

Watching your weight? Swap out the pita bread in this recipe for plain rice cakes.

Serves 6

Ingredients
1 tablespoon fresh-minced ginger

3 cloves garlic

½ teaspoon soy sauce

1 tablespoon sesame oil

¼ cup sesame seeds

1 pound fresh tuna steak

1 apple, any type

1 bunch scallions

6 rice cakes

1. Mix together the ginger, garlic, soy, ½ tablespoon sesame oil, and the sesame seeds. Encrust the tuna with the seed mixture.

2. Heat a sauté pan on highest heat; sear the outside of the tuna very quickly. Wrap the tuna in plastic wrap and freeze solid.

3. Remove from plastic wrap and, using a very sharp knife, slice the tuna as thinly as possible. Thinly slice the apple and slice the scallions on an extreme bias.

4. Brush the rice cakes with the rest of the sesame oil, and layer with tuna, apple, and scallions.

Potato Salad Lettuce Rolls

Dried herbs are usually okay to use when a recipe calls for fresh, but remember that dried herbs are much more potent than fresh. Plan to use less.

Serves 6

Ingredients

6 cooked Idaho potatoes or 12 small red-skinned potatoes

½ bulb roasted garlic

1 yellow onion

¼ cup extra-virgin olive oil

2 tablespoons balsamic vinegar

¼ bunch parsley, chopped

Fresh-cracked black pepper

Kosher salt

1 head large-leaf lettuce

1. Chop the potatoes and mash them with the garlic.

2. Mix together all the ingredients except the lettuce. Adjust seasoning to taste.

3. Place the potato salad on lettuce leaves, then roll up.